Not Waiting on My Boaz: Winning in My Singleness

Dedra D. Colston

ISBN: 979-8-8465-5971-4

CONTENTS

ACKNOWLEDGMENTS

Thank you to my mother, best friend, and girlfriends for listening to my woes, sitting with me while I cried, and being my accountability partner. Thank you for your prayers, counsel, and advice. Thank you for checking me when I was out of the will of God and pointing me back to the word of God to ground me in my decisions. Thank you for allowing me to be there for you to do the same! Thank you for the laughs, the stories, and our made for tv dramas. We all have a singlehood story to tell, and because of our experiences, I hope to bless, encourage, and motivate others as you all have done for me!

INTRODUCTION

I know the title has you wondering, "What is she about to write? Of course, I am waiting for my Boaz, but let's see where she goes with this." I, too, was wondering about this title when God dropped it into my spirit in 2018. I was at work minding my own business when I picked up my pencil and scribbled the title. I took a perplexed glance at it after writing, cocked my head to the side, and said, "Okay, Lord! I don't know what it will be about, but I trust you." So here I am three and a half years later. It has been a slow process to understand what God wants to say through me to all of you, those who are single, divorced, and widowed. It has taken me three years to focus on what to be transparent about and what I feel comfortable sharing. It has been four years since I entered a relationship out of my dry season of singlehood, and finally, it is all coming together.

Sometimes we see being single as a curse, a horrible place to be. Other times we view it as freedom, the ability to not worry about anyone but ourselves, going, traveling, and living as we please. But being single is NOT for the weak. It is a trying place some days. It is a lonely place some days. It is a bitter place some days. It is a triumphant place some days, and it is always, without fail, a reflective place every day! I am a 40-plus-year-old woman who has never been married and has had few monogamous relationships. Of course, I have dated here and there, but nothing was ever solid nor led anywhere. I was, in a sense, settled on the fact that I would be "single." Yes, I prayed for a relationship, a wonderful Godly man, all that good stuff, but I had become "okay" with being ALONE. However, in 2018, after a lot of prayers, I told my mom that I was finally CONTENT with where I was in life as a single woman. I no longer cared about a relationship or marriage. I only wanted to become a foster parent, love a child (although deep down, I wanted to birth my own), do what God placed on my heart to do, and live life.

Well, God is always listening. He not only listens to our hearts, but He knows our desires or deepest wants and will bless us when He sees we are ready! This book is about me, you, being prepared for what we have been praying for and desire. It is about checking where we are in life and positioning ourselves to receive what He has for us. It is about Him perfecting our hurt, disappointment, pain, and trauma. It is about grounding us in the word and learning to honor God in all we do. It is about making God first, not last, in our relationships with others. It is about winning in our singleness and owning who we are. It is about growing and maturing in our walk, so we are ready to be submissive, yes, submissive in our marriage. It is about spending devoted time with God and walking in our purpose. It is about loving ourselves in our entirety, understanding our needs, and knowing what we won't put up with and genuinely want.

Not Waiting on My Boaz is not a book about finding a man, searching for a man, or waiting on a man. It is about identifying your needs, wants, and desires. It is about maturing in your thinking and actions. It is about becoming content in your singleness and loving every minute. It is about readying yourself for the blessings God has in store for you, so let's jump in! What does it mean to be single? Well, as I learned in the pre-marital class, I attended, being single refers to one who is "not married." Yep, being single in the context of this book will mean that you are unmarried, whether in a dating relationship, non-dating relationship, divorced, or widowed. You are now single. How does that make you feel? Does it put you on defense, especially those in a relationship? Does it bring up any emotions for you?

I know I have become resigned to understanding that I am single until married, so hearing that does not affect me nor make me feel singled out. It does not bring up any negative emotions in me. I am content with it, and I believe it is due to attending that pre-marital class as a single woman many moons ago. It made me realize I had a lot of work on internally. At the time, I was so into wanting a man. I desired to date, be in a relationship, get married, and have a child. I was in my early 30s and had enough of being alone. So, I decided to find out if I was ready to "settle down." Well, that answer was a resounding, "NO!" I quickly learned I had issues understanding what being submissive meant and was not ready to compromise. I left that class and never returned, and from that point forward, I began to work on Dedra.

My takeaway was that although I knew what marriage looked like from the outside, I was not ready to do the work on the inside to keep it alive. As a single person, it is easy for us to walk away from a relationship when specific tests and trials come. I believe that to be successful in the end game of marriage, we must be successful in our singlehood. So, prepare your heart to receive from God. Prepare to dig deep, reflect on what the Holy Spirit reveals to you on this journey, and welcome this opportunity for growth and maturity.

Chapter 1

Ruth & Boaz: Not Your Average Love Story

"Then she fell on her face, bowing to the ground, and said to him, "Why have I found favor in your eyes that you should notice me, when I am a foreigner?"
-Ruth 2:10

In the beginning

We all know the story of Ruth, or so we think. Preachers, pastors, and evangelists have taught this chapter from the perspective of Ruth being "found" by Boaz; however, when you read the chapter and understand the time, culture, and background, you fully grasp the love story of Ruth, Naomi, and Boaz. Let's dig in and understand Ruth, Naomi (Mara), and Boaz's story and learn what we can take from it to apply to our relationships.

In the first chapter of Ruth, Elimelech and his family moved to Moab due to a drought in Bethlehem. While in Moab for ten years, Elimelech dies and Naomi's sons marry two Moabite women, Orpah and Ruth. The union between the sons and the Moabite women was classified as an unequally yoked union because Moabites were Gentiles with different beliefs and worshipped different gods, not the God of Abraham. But, as fate would have it, Naomi's sons die, and all three women become destitute. Naomi decides to return home with no skills or way to make a living, and her daughters-in-law's journey with her after hearing living conditions are better in Bethlehem. As they journey to Bethlehem, Naomi begins to feel she would hold Orpah and Ruth back due to her age and that Bethlehem would be a foreign land to Orpah and Ruth. Naomi urges Orpah and Ruth to return to their families, as they are young and still of child-bearing age and able to have another family. Orpah eventually agrees to Naomi's pleas, but Ruth decides to stay with her mother-in-law and go to a foreign land to help support her. Ruth proves her loyalty by turning from her "worldly" environment to follow Naomi and placing her faith and trust in the God Naomi worships. In chapter one, Ruth possesses qualities we can take on, loyalty and faithfulness. Her decision to leave her past behind speaks volumes about how we, as single women, must move forward. We cannot become stuck in a past life or relationship believing that that is all there is for us. We must decide to move forward, cultivate relationships with other women who love God, and work on our relationship with God by trusting and having faith in the moves He makes in our lives.

As we move into Chapter 2, we learn that Naomi is mourning her losses and changes her name to Mara (bitter) due to all that has happened to her, but she realizes Ruth can help provide for them. Side note: Sometimes, we need a Naomi in our life to set us up for the win, and this is what Naomi does. Naomi and Ruth enter Bethlehem during harvest season, and according to law, farmers were to skip the edges of grain fields and leave some grapes on the vine for the poor and foreigners to reap. "And you shall not glean your vineyard bare, neither shall you gather its fallen grapes; you shall leave them for the poor and the stranger. I am the Lord your God." (Leviticus 19:10). Knowing the law, Naomi sends Ruth to her relative, Boaz's field, to glean. Here is where the sermons get us with, "Boaz saw her working," but fail to say, Naomi, sets up Ruth. Naomi knew the law. She knew that a relative of her husband could marry the widow of his dead relative. She knew that Ruth was young and beautiful and that Boaz was wealthy. The WIN set-up! Naomi was going to ensure someone would care for them! Boaz returns from his travels and "sees"

Ruth working in his fields, begins to ask questions about her and finds out that Ruth has initiative and is hard-working. He sees these qualities in her and tells her to work in his fields from there on out. Ruth 2:5, "Then Boaz said to his servant who was set over the reapers, Whose maidservant is this?"

The lesson here is that, as single women, we should be concerned about fulfilling kingdom purpose and fulfilling our passions and dreams because if you desire a mate, he will watch how you move and conduct yourself, always without YOU noticing. He then gives her directions on how to glean and informs Ruth that he has protected her from other men who might try to harm her. Boaz is exhibiting the qualities of being a provider and protector, which is what you need if you desire a mate. Ruth is taken aback and asks why he has shown her favor. Again, Boaz has done his homework and tells Ruth that he knows how she has left her homeland to take care of Naomi and has remained loyal to her in a foreign land, and this is where the love story begins.

Ruth's focus was not on "getting a man," "securing the bag," or "getting married." Naomi had a plan to ensure their provisions by sending Ruth to a field where she would be "seen" by Boaz, and Naomi's plan worked. Boaz took notice of Ruth's work ethic and loyalty to her mother-in-law, not just her beauty. He saw the true essence of Ruth because Ruth was just herself, and then the plot thickens. Ruth broke bread and worked until the end of the day and, upon her return home, showed Naomi her reaping for the day. Naomi feigns ignorant and asks Ruth where she worked. Naomi's heart is overjoyed after Ruth tells her, and after hearing Boaz's name, she tells Ruth who Boaz is and how he can redeem them, encouraging her to continue to listen to Boaz's instructions through the end of the harvest season.

In chapter 3, Naomi sets them up for the home run! By this time, Ruth and Boaz have probably formed a working relationship, and feelings have grown. He has seen her continual support of Naomi and her work ethic, and she has seen his continual kindness and generosity towards her. Naomi tells Ruth to put on perfume, get dressed up, and go to Boaz's threshing floor, but do not make herself known until he is full of eating and drinking. Then, once Boaz had laid down for the night, Ruth was to place herself at his feet, signifying her desire to be redeemed by Boaz. When Boaz awakens to find her at his feet, Ruth makes her intentions known by asking Boaz to spread your wing [of protection] over your maidservant, for you are a next of kin. Ruth 3:10-11, and his reply, and he said, 10 "And he said, Blessed be you of the Lord, my daughter. For you have made this last loving-kindness greater than the former, for you have not gone after young men, whether poor or rich. 11 And now, my daughter, fear not. I will do for you all you require, for all my people in the city know that you are a woman of strength (worth, bravery, capability)." From this point, the wheels begin moving, and Boaz sets his plan in motion to make Ruth his wife but realizes that he is not the next of kin to marry Ruth and tells her this.

Finally, in Chapter 4, Boaz takes ten elders with him to speak to the relative next in line to purchase Elimelech's land and redeem Naomi. Boaz lets him know that Elimelech is deceased, and Naomi has returned with her widowed daughter-in-law, who is a Moabite. He tells his relative that if he takes on Elimelech's land, he must also redeem Naomi and Ruth, but Boaz already knows that no other man would take a Moabite woman as his wife as they could forfeit their inheritance. The next of kin denies the land and the redemption of Naomi and Ruth, passes it on to Boaz, and the elders bless Boaz and Ruth's union. Boaz returns and marries Ruth, and they give birth to Obed, the father of Jesse, the father of David, the ancestors of Christ!

The story of Ruth and Boaz was no average love story. This story is about loss, loyalty, compassion, generosity, kindness, and redemption. It is a story of triumph in darkness when all seems bleak. It is a story of second chances! The love story was not just about Boaz seeing Ruth or Ruth seeing Boaz as someone who would redeem her and Naomi; it was about Ruth loving Naomi enough to leave her past behind, learn about God, and her conversion to Judaism. It was about Ruth putting her mother-in-law before herself and listening to her to help secure their future. It was about Boaz noticing a woman, researching her past, and deciding he would provide and protect Ruth. When pastors teach this Bible book, they do not take the time to stress the qualities and characteristics of Ruth or her love towards Naomi; to me, that is the true love story here.

Ruth was a widowed, single woman who was trustworthy, obedient, loyal, faithful, hard-working, and honest. She was concerned with ensuring her mother-in-law was cared for and that they had provisions. Ruth was concerned about fulfilling her purpose and survival, not "getting a man," and in her pursuit of caring for Naomi, she had someone else working behind the scenes to place her where she needed to be "seen." Quite often, single women position themselves to receive attention. Whose attention are we seeking? Do any of these men have

Boaz's characteristics or qualities? Are they ensuring your survival, providing for, and protecting you at all costs?

Our primary concern as single women should be spending time with God and fulfilling our purpose because our attention is not divided or concentrated on our husbands during this time. 1 Corinthians 7: 34, "And the unmarried woman or girl is concerned and anxious about the matters of the Lord, how to be wholly separated and set apart in body and spirit; but the married woman has her cares [centered] in earthly affairs how she may please her husband." God sets you up to be SEEN by whom he has designed for you! That's it, and that's all in a nutshell! So, when we hear the sermons on Ruth and Boaz, we know that this love story was not cut and dry. It is a story of heartache, pain, a renewed spirit, purpose, loyalty, and LOVE!

Ruth & Boaz: Not Your Average Love Story Reflections

What personal qualities/traits do you possess, and how do those qualities/traits affect your relationships?

If dating as a single, divorced, or widowed woman, what is your primary focus in a relationship? If you are not dating, what would be your primary focus?

Do you surround yourself with a circle of women who provide accountability, motivation, and counsel? If yes, why, and how does it help you? If not, why not, and how can you change this?

Read the Chapter of Ruth. What did you learn from Ruth and Naomi's relationship? How can their relationship help you build and maintain relationships with other women?

After reading Ruth, what did you learn about Naomi, Ruth, and Boaz? How can their attributes, relationships, and work ethics help shape your thoughts, desires, and personal growth moving forward?

Chapter 2

The Alice in Wonderland Saga

"Who are you?"
- the Caterpillar

Fairytales and Nightmares

That seems to be what most of our dating relationships are. When I was younger, I imagined I would be married to a great man who would love our kids like my dad modeled for me, but here I am in my mid 40's, and all I have are journal pages filled with love, drama, and heartache with little glimmers of hope! Like many single, divorced, and widowed women's love stories, my love story is filled with ups, downs, and traveling down roads most traveled but always filled with the unknown. I know that dating has not always been easy for me, nor some of you. I tend to keep things very close to my chest because, as most of you know, the more you give, the more someone will take, which can sometimes destroy you emotionally, mentally, and spiritually.

Most women are nurturers and tend to want to heal and help the person we are in a dating or romantic relationship. We give our all and deal with their trauma and drama, thinking, if I can get the person to see things how I see them, he will be better. But let's be honest, dating is not for the faint at heart. It is taking a risk and having an open heart to receive what you believe love is in hopes of reciprocity. Sometimes, this happens, which is that fairytale some of us think of or journal. The fairytale of planned dates, no drama, open communication, trust, honesty, fun, adventure, and all the highs you could imagine. On the other hand, it can be a total nightmare consisting of drama, lies, betrayal, uncertainty, misrepresentation, and abuse; when we continue this rollercoaster called love, it can and will sometimes leave us bitter and in a dry place.

I liken my relationship history to Alice in Wonderland. The characters, or men, I have met have taken me down the rabbit hole of lust, love, drama, and pain, which caused me to question who I was and what I had to give, and many women have been in this place. It has most definitely been an adventure, and the stories are PRICELESS! I am sure you, too, have crazy dating stories. Stories of meeting men who presented themselves as secure, having it all together, ready to do the dangum thang with you, but you soon realize it was all a façade. Or maybe you fell in lust thinking it was love and got married only to learn the person was only showing you his "representative." You know the person you gave specific details of the man you desire in your many conversations.

The "ideal" guy with the characteristics and qualities of your knight in shining armor, only to find out he isn't anything he portrays. He lied and deceived you, and now you are in a position of having to decide what you will do. Do you trust the possibility of him becoming the "representative"? Do you put up with the fakeness and lies, or do you walk away? Sadly, many women choose option two hoping to transform the man into option one. Ladies, it does not work and creates a vicious cycle of emotional pain for you. This emotional pain is fertile ground for low self-esteem and lack of confidence; this is how we lose ourselves, our identity!

My dating adventures have been downright sad. I seemed never to get it right, or so I thought. My experiences include being "stood up," meeting a man I thought would be better than the rest, dating the "church" guy who was no different from the average street guy, to talking to a single husband. Yes, a single husband- a married man portraying himself as a single man. The list could go on and on, but many of my dating adventures were not pleasant.

One day, I read through my journals and cried. I cried and was angry reading about my dating disappointments and the things I chose to allow. I once dated a gentleman that met me when I was in one of those "depressed" states. He did not know this, but I was not in a place to date; however, the "attention" seemed to ease my sadness. He appeared to have it together; a decent job he was successful in, a home, believed in God and went to church, loved to do, and experience new things, and was into saving and investing. The list could go on and on about all the "GREAT" qualities he possessed, but he was a Dr. Jekyll and Mr. Hyde. Yep, he had a personality disorder; I diagnosed him with one, as counseling is my background, but I'm not sure. He knew how to make me feel great, supported, and heard. He wanted, or so I believed, to be more than just "friends with benefits," which was the type of relationship I desired.

He was attentive and caring and always wanted to ensure I was good. BUT he had an ugly side, and that side made me question myself more times than I should have, and when there comes a time when we no longer recognize ourselves, we must learn to let go and move on. He would lash out at odd times and speak to me disrespectfully. He would allow his friends to talk about me in disrespectful ways and would laugh with them. He would act like it was a hassle for him to drive to my side of town to visit me or give subliminal messages about what other women in his past and probably present were doing for him. He would start arguments, and when I barked back, he would say I was overreacting.

The sad thing is that I held on to the relationship for a few years, knowing I did not need to be in it. Why? I was in a place of being upset with myself for not being able to maintain a relationship. I felt I was the one getting it wrong. How many times have you felt like you were getting it wrong? Although I knew it was not me, I still blamed myself for not being able to sustain a relationship. How often have you talked yourself into staying with someone who dishonored or was verbally, physically, or emotionally abusive to you? I once did and knew it was not of my character; therefore, it came to the point of taking care of myself and letting go of what was not working, and I chose myself.

You see, our nightmare relationships show us who we are not! Those relationships test us beyond being tested and tend to do serious work on our psyche. We sometimes change in character for the good or bad, believing we are the person who exists in these warped relationships. We allow the lies, deceit, and irrational behavior to continue at times due to not wanting to be "single" again. Still, some of you are reading this saying, "I would never," although you have nine times out of ten. These types of relationships should grow and mature us. They should show us how much strength we have and outline what we need if we recognize that the relationship is not suitable for us. However, sometimes, our self-esteem and confidence become so destroyed that we allow ourselves to stay in this abusive relationship because we feel we need it, and that is a LIE from the depths of HELL! God did not position man as our "head" to abuse and mistreat us. The man should treat us as Christ loves the church, and if the man we desire to be our husband is not doing that, we must learn to let him go.

On the flip side, we have those relationships we deem "fairytales." You know, the relationship where everything seems to be going smoothly. The man you are dating is kind and responsive, tries to communicate, plans, and surprises you with dates. He gives you all of him by being transparent, and things are smooth. However, three months turn into six, six months turn into nine, and nine months lead to two years, and nothing has progressed. He continues to string you along, insisting you "move in" together. He has become complacent and does not do any of the things he did from the beginning to "win" you over, and you become somewhat tired and, fed up, begin to voice your feelings, and things go awry. How many of you have traveled this road? My "so-called" fairytale was an on-again, off-again relationship; friends and family knew me, and I thought we were solid until a significant life change happened, and things did not look the same anymore. My fairytale was coming to an end, but not for another ten years.

I held onto the pseudo-relationship because it was familiar. I dated other people in the meantime but held out for the fairytale ending that Mariah Carey sang about in her song, Butterfly. That song was my word! If I believed in what the song said, then my fairytale was to be, and he would return, but sadly I was the one who had to cut it off. As much as I wanted that relationship to succeed, I had to hear it from the horse's mouth. As women, we must realize we have the power to let go. Yes, it will hurt, but we must get out of the Alice in

Wonderland craziness.

We allow many things to happen in relationships by not speaking up. We allow specific treatment to go on because we fear losing someone, but the reality is that that person does not belong in our lives anymore! I asked my fairytale a straightforward question, "Do you want to be with me or ever want to be with me?" He tried to give this, "you're a good woman, and I love you speech," but ladies, keep them focused. I asked again and simply said, "this is a yes or no question." I already knew the answer, but to truly let go, you must hear it yourself. My fairytale said, "no," and I was so crushed. Not because we would not be together, but because I had wasted my time for many years thinking he would come around. Were there signs? Yes! There are always signs, but how many of us genuinely heed them?

The Alice in Wonderland sagas make us feel like we are in the dating world trying to win one! It gives us excitement, conversation, days to look forward to, drama, love, and connection! It is a love-hate experience that we all know too well. We complain about the "representatives" and how they do us wrong. We cry over the fairytales and nightmares, hoping they will do better or change after this day or time. Some of us put up with deceit and lies because it gives us someone to talk to and "feel" special. But the main question from these experiences is, "Who are YOU"? Whom are you becoming during these relationships? Does this person line up with who you are? Whom have you become due to this relationship, and how is it affecting your relationship with God and others?

We cannot allow our dramas and disappointments in our fairytales, nor our nightmares, to dictate who we are. We cannot lose ourselves in the "new" person we become due to hurt, pain, or disappointment. We are "fearfully and wonderfully" made! We must learn to use discernment and wisdom in our relationships and rely on God to dictate our path of whom we allow or not allow in our life. Stop participating in the Alice in Wonderland adventures, and let God lead you on your journey!

The Alice in Wonderland Saga Reflections

Who are you? Think about your characteristics, talents, likes, and dislikes, and summarize who you are in CHRIST.

Have you ever allowed a relationship to dictate who you were? If so, why? How did you change? How did this affect your self-esteem/confidence"?

Based on your previous experiences, how will you navigate dating differently in the future?

List two scriptures you can meditate on to remind you of WHO you are and WHOM you belong.
Scripture 1:
Scripture 2:

Chapter 3

God, Are You There?

"Search me, O God, and know my heart; try me, and know my thoughts."
-Psalms 139:3

God, I NEED you!

How many times have you asked this question during a relationship or after? What led to this question or cry? I know for myself; it was the cycle of dating men and constantly feeling "let down" time and again! It was the feeling of defeat, and the nagging feeling of "this cannot be what is out there for me?" I have listened to "relationship" experts and gurus say, "you attract what or who you are," and to be honest, that is FAR from the truth for me! I am not a manipulator, liar, cheater, user, or adulterer. I am not TOXIC or abusive. I simply care too much and want things to work out; however, that does not mean I do not have flaws.

As I stated in the previous chapter, our past or current relationships leave marks on us that we sometimes have difficulty removing and, in the process, create insecurities. We allow comments that shape us and destroy our self-esteem and confidence. We begin to believe that we are inadequate and not deserving of a better relationship and partner. We allow the failed relationship or divorce to birth bitterness; this is not what God designed us for, nor is it the reality of who we are! So, let's dig in! My question to you is, WHO ARE YOU? Whom have you allowed yourself to become due to your past relationships? Is this whom God says you are?

Depending on the relationship or person, we naturally tend to transform in some way or another. In some of my past relationships, I have had to check myself and say, "Dedra, this is not you! Why are you allowing this person to treat you this way?" This recognition was not immediate but a slow realization that

I was becoming stressed and not feeling confident. It was the negative self-talk I would have with myself and the minor changes I was making to create allowances for this person to continue to exist in "my world." All of this led to feelings of inadequacy and defeat. I was allowing the thought of "I was not enough" to take over my decisions, and failure would creep in as the thought of being unable to sustain a relationship. Although I know it takes two to make something work, I began to make it all about why I could not get it right, and this created problems and cycles for me. In our thoughts of not being enough or being able to "get it right," let's look at the word inadequacy.

Inadequacy:

1) the state or quality of being inadequate; lack of the quantity or quality required
2) inability to deal with a situation or with life (Oxford Languages).

I want you to consider this definition and how it applies to different areas of your life. Now, I want you to think about how you have allowed the thought of inadequacy to direct your actions and decisions. Our society does a great job of making us feel inadequate daily, for example, people on social media post ideal pictures of their relationships with the perfect hashtag or images of women with enhancements and no flaws. We are beaten down with the notion that if you are not like "this" or do not have "that," then you are not on track, hence, inadequate. But that is not your truth.

The truth is that we are human and take in what is around us. We compare ourselves against a false narrative and try our best to reach, at times, an unattainable goal. We compare ourselves and our relationships to others, and when we do not obtain the level of what we think we should attain, we feel defeated and inadequate. Think about the hashtag #relationshipgoals. The hashtag is full of perfect photos, smiles, hand holding, date nights, exotic trips, etc.; you get the point. Now, suppose you have not been in a stable and secure relationship. You might take this information, measure against it, try to implement what these people have done or are pushing, or make a conclusion that is not true about yourself. We must understand that these imperfect people create perfect photo shots, shows, and podcasts about how their relationship works and what is best for them, pushing their experiences and opinions as facts.

Remember Jada Pinkett-Smith and her Red Table talk with Will when the August Alsina fiasco transpired? That situation was an entire mess, but if you are one hooked on #relationshipgoals and how people present themselves on social media, you were probably disappointed to find out that Will and Jada are not exactly #relationshipgoals, or how about Ciara? I remember when Ciara talked about the prayer she prayed for her husband and how all-over social media, women were saying, "I need to pray her prayer." Crazy, right? Ciara had been in a few failed relationships that probably left her raw, vulnerable, and possibly insecure or feeling inadequate. She probably realized that her relationships had specific patterns and needed to make a change for the better. Ciara realized that the only one who can ensure her "BOAZ" is God, not her friends or the world. Ciara's "God, are you there and need you moment" became a prayer for God to search her heart, bless her with what she needed, and guide the relationship. Society, social media to be exact, will lead some of us to constantly compare our relationships to other people's standards which will always have one asking, "God, are you there?" Why? Because we are not aligning our thoughts and desires to God's for our relationships but looking towards the world, which leads to us feeling inadequate or defeated.

On the other hand, we get involved with men who are not supposed to be in our lives at all. We "allow" (I want you to say that word out loud, ALLOW) certain behaviors to "keep" the man so that we do not feel alone. We settle, which we will talk about later, and hold on for dear life because we do not want to be ALONE, and this all leads to feelings of insecurity, hurt, and defeat. In each relationship, I have been in, or whenever I would begin dating someone, I would pray for God to reveal to me what needed to be seen, if this person should be in my presence, and to give me a sign if I was doing what He wanted me to do. But guess what? Although I prayed this prayer and sought God, I ended up staying where I knew I did not belong because I was tired of not getting it right or being alone. I was responsible for my feelings of defeat, of my "God, are you there" moments, because I chose to stay way past the expiration date of the relationship, and I know I am not alone in this.

Many of you also stayed when you knew it was time to leave. We have all remained for various reasons and allowed the negative to continue. We let the hurt continue. We have allowed the pain to continue and the feelings of being inadequate to be cast upon us because we were not ready to let go when we needed to. As women and daughters of God, we must know that we are jewels in His crown and deserve the best, but we cannot have the best when we refuse to let go when it is time. God has never failed us in our "God, are you there" feelings of defeat moments. No, God is always there listening, watching, and hoping we listen to what the Holy Spirit is trying to speak to us. God is always there waiting on us to come to Him. We must remember that He will never leave us nor forsake us, but we have a significant role in the decisions that we make for ourselves.

To you who feel inadequate in your current relationship, ask yourself why you are still there. To you who feel defeated by one failed relationship after the other, ask yourself what the common denominator or problem is. To the women lacking self-confidence, ask yourself what happened or was said to make you feel uncertain. To you who hate to be alone, ask yourself why you are not comfortable with your own company.

We have work to do, ladies! We must know, without a doubt, that God only wants the best for us, but we have a hand in ensuring we are aligned and connected to the right person. Today marks the last day of ALLOWING a relationship to dictate how you feel about yourself, ALLOWING a man to tell you your worth, and ALLOWING just anyone to entertain you. You deserve more and can have it! Today, make yourself a PRIORITY!

God, Are You There?
Reflections

How have you allowed a relationship to transform you?

What comment(s) from a current or past relationship has left marks on your self-esteem or confidence?

What changes have you made to "fit" or "allow" a person to exist in your world?

What situations or circumstances have led to a "God, are you there?" moment?

In what ways do you feel inadequate or not enough?

Whom does God say that you are?

Find 5-8 verses to meditate on when you begin to feel defeated or inadequate. Post these scriptures where you can see them daily.

Chapter 4

You Aren't Dust, So Stop Settling!

"The minute you settle for less than you deserve,
you get even less than you settled for."
-Maureen Dowd

Remember, dust settles, not you

Let's face it, settling comes from a place of desperation and deciding to give up. When we think about settling, one has become resolved to tolerate whatever is happening in the relationship because you don't believe you can do better, deserve better, or are willing to hold on to what you have because of the fear of starting over again. Settling can mean many other things to many people, but at the end of the day, it all comes to the one meaning of GIVING UP on what we need and what our heart desires! I liken our relationships to dust settling because dust is not suitable for anyone, just like some of our relationships. Dust is a collection of hair, dead skin, mites, and other allergens and particles that is not good for us to inhale. Did you catch that? Dust is not beneficial and is a collection of harmful things.

Ladies, your decision to "settle" is all on you. It is a conscious decision to go outside the will of God to pursue what is not good and healthy. I want you to think of a time when going outside God's will was good for you. The relationships you enter may seem decent and pleasurable initially, but why do you choose to stay when you see signs of controlling behavior, abuse, cheating, manipulation, destructive behavior, and untrustworthiness? What has caused you to become desensitized to the ill-treatment you are receiving? What in you is allowing you to just go with the flow?

God created us to be winners, a blessing, and live in prosperity, but when we decide that we deserve what we are getting, we have failed and are not walking in victory! As a single woman, you must recognize the difference between what someone is giving you to fulfill a checklist you have and what you truly deserve, which leads to answering the following questions to check your mindset. Do you know what type of love you deserve; can you describe it in detail and use it as a base to measure your relationships? I want you to think back to your childhood. Some of us had father figures in our homes, and some did not.

If you lived in a two-parent household, what characteristics of love did you witness your father giving to your mother? How was she treated? How was love expressed towards you and or your siblings? I know for myself; that my father was very protective and loving. He worked hard to support our home and provide for our needs. He loved my mother and was visible in showing us that love towards her daily. He hugged and listened to her. He respected her input, prayed with her, and honored her. Even when they argued, they respected my brother and me enough to do it behind closed doors, and when those doors opened, they still showed love for one another.

My father gave me an "earthly" basc of what love looks and feels like from a man. He was my example of what I deserved and what I needed. Therefore, when I began dating, I voiced if I saw signs of anything opposed to what I knew I should receive. Some men took stock of what I said, and others said my mouth was too much or I was sassy, and with those types of comments, I knew that the person was not for me. But, in my younger years, knowing what I needed was sometimes overshadowed by my wants, leading me to settle. The desperation on my part to maintain a relationship that was noticeably outside the will of God and not in alignment with what I knew I needed was me settling, and I always recognized it. The young Dedra "wanted" what she wanted, and now, older and wiser, I see all the hurt and pain I, let me repeat it, "I," caused myself because I was raised and saw differently.

On the other hand, maybe a father was not in the home. Instead, you use your mother's interactions with men as a base for your relationship. A relationship that could sometimes be short, on and off again, abusive, needy, manipulative, one-sided, and toxic, is all you know. Maybe due to the poor relationships you witnessed growing up, you believe that you take what you can get and just "deal" with the person because they are giving you what you "want," not necessarily "need." Maybe they are fulfilling the absence of not having an earthly male figure role that you so desired growing up, and now, as an adult, you hold onto what you believe you need, although recognizing that it is hurtful and harmful to you. However, you settle in it because you do not know anything else.

Well, sisters, I am here to tell you that our Father did not create us to settle for less. Deciding to settle means you agree that you do not deserve more. Jeremiah 29:11, "For I know the thoughts and *plans* I have for you, says the Lord, thoughts *and* plans for welfare *and* peace and not for evil, to give you hope in your final outcome." When we decide to settle for less, we are essentially telling God we do not deserve His best! God did not create us to lose in life nor take the least. He designed us to prosper in all areas of our life, including our relationships. When we settle for the least with our partners, this can affect how we allow others to treat us daily. We rationalize and begin to believe the lie the enemy is attempting to and, at times, succeeds in telling us. When we accept defeat, we birth low self-esteem and low self-confidence. We must give our relationships back to the ONE who can bless or dismiss them and learn to be okay with the outcome. We must know what is good for us by reading God's word.

1 Corinthians 13: 4-8 is the only example of what love is. It is the blueprint for what love looks like and what we should demand from ourselves, not just our partners. In your single season, wholly love yourself and know the type of love you desire. 1 Corinthians 13:4-8, 4 "love endures *and* is patient and kind; love never is envious *nor* boils over with jealousy, is not boastful *or* vainglorious, does not display itself haughtily. 5 It is not conceited (arrogant and inflated with pride); it is not rude (unmannerly) *and* does not act unbecomingly. Love (God's love in us) does not insist on its own rights *or* its own way, *for* it is not self-seeking; it is not touchy *or* fretful *or* resentful; it takes no account of the evil done to it [it pays no attention to a suffered wrong]. 6 It does not rejoice at injustice *and* unrighteousness but rejoices when right *and* truth prevail. 7 Love bears up under anything *and* everything that comes, is ever ready to believe the best of every person, its hopes are fadeless under all circumstances, and it endures everything [without weakening]. 8 Love never fails [never fades out or becomes obsolete or comes to an end]." This scripture explains that love is not designed to hurt. Love is forgiving, uplifting, supportive, helpful, honest, and ever-growing. It is not abusive or misleading. Love is reciprocated and not filled with one-sided affection. Love is not settling for what you hope to get, but it is getting

what you deserve and much more!

As you continue to walk in your singleness, know that you must learn to love yourself more than any man on Earth can. You must know what kind of love you deserve and need, not want. You must demand to be treated like Christ loves the church, whole, without conceit and unwavering. You must not settle like dust, collecting all the unhealthy particles that lead to toxic thoughts, feelings, and behaviors. Today, decide to love you more! Today, decide to let go of what is not God's best for you! Today, choose to stop going with your heart, and rely on your spirit to lead you to your BEST! Today, remember to tell yourself I love you and will never settle for second best!

You Aren't Dust, So Stop Settling!
Reflections

What does love look like to you?

Who are your examples of a healthy relationship? What are the characteristics of their relationship? How does it shape your view of what to accept in a relationship?

Why did you settle in your past relationship? How are you currently settling in your current relationship? Explain why.

How has settling affected how you view yourself? Reread 1 Corinthians 13: 4-8. What is it saying to you about how love looks? How can you use these verses to aid you in your future relationships?

Chapter 5

Girl, Get Yourself Together!

"It's time to focus on you."
-Dedra Colston

Working on ME is the ultimate VICTORY!

Many times, we are so focused on "getting a man," "being in a relationship," or "what went wrong in the relationship" that we never put in the same energy to focus on ourselves to better who we are. We spend time preparing ourselves for what we think a man wants or desires instead of pouring into ourselves the things we need to be whole. The worst thing any woman can do is not know who she is, what she wants, desires, and needs. A woman will quickly head toward destruction when she spends more time on her outer than inner self. I see posts, blogs, and even TV shows where women are shapeshifting to fit the mold of what society says a "woman" should be or look like or what the man they are dating feels she should be. I watch shows where broken women use their sexual prowess to get what they want, no matter whom they hurt or how they continue to hurt themselves. I see women who are missing a mother or father figure or a healthy relationship with a parent and do not know what healthy love looks like due to that loss.

Knowing who you are and whose you are is so vital. We are lost when we do not know who or whose we are, plain and simple. We attach to anything or anyone who makes us feel important and look for love in all the wrong places. We put relationships with others before ourselves. We never learn what it means to value ourselves, our bodies, and our minds. Preparing and focusing on yourself and your purpose is vital before pouring your all into another person. A woman who does not know herself will accept, believe, and do anything to garner the attention and love of a person whose love, at best, is conditional.

Let's face it. Love can be conditional, especially when someone senses that you do not know your self-worth. When you are strong, know who and whose you are; no person can belittle nor make you feel unworthy. The most important thing I learned from attending pre-marital counseling as a single woman with no man was that I was unprepared. I was so focused on being in a relationship that I was not working on Dedra, the woman, the prospective wife, and the mother. I was just living, doing my thing. I was not even focused on ministry as I should have been. That class opened my eyes and taught me a valuable lesson about preparation. So, let's dig in and prepare yourself, not for marriage, but ministry and purpose!

I have a question; do you know who you are? I know that may seem like a weird question, but do you? Do you know what makes you tick? Do you know what your weaknesses are, and have you begun working on strengthening them? Are you comfortable in your skin, just how you are? Do you have insecurities? Have you been hurt by someone and need healing? What areas need healing? Many of you will say no, so it's time to do some surgery! You must learn to love who you are before you expect a man to do so!

God created you specifically to glorify his name. He crafted and molded you to be whom He designed you to be. He created us to be wonderful beings! Psalm 139:13-14, "For You did form my inward parts; You did knit me together in my mother's womb. 14 I will confess and praise You for You are fearful and wonderful and for the awful wonder of my birth! Wonderful are Your works, and that my inner self knows right well."

These verses are critical to our self-worth. God created us to be jewels in His crown, nothing less! I firmly believe that before we get involved in a relationship, we must know and love who we are. In this forever stage of preparation, you must know you, love you, and ensure your best interests are always first. What does love yourself mean? It means loving every part of you, even the areas you feel are undesirable. Loving yourself is crucial because when you lack self-confidence and self-esteem, it is easy for a man to twist your vision of yourself into what he believes you are. A warped idea of yourself leads to being someone you are not, which is detrimental to your mental wellness. It will become easy to place value on what others say about you than what you think or say about yourself. It is always taking someone's words and giving them power over you, and that is not of God.

God created you to be uniquely you. He created you to look how you look and possess the characteristics that make you, you. It was no mistake. I am not saying you cannot choose to improve parts of yourself, but if you are doing it to measure up to society's ideals or what you feel a man desires, this is erroneous thinking. You should love yourself enough and be in tune with your needs to know what you need to improve or work on, such as healing from a past relationship, brokenness from your upbringing, or lack of self-esteem or confidence. We must learn to do the internal work of healing and growing before even thinking about being in a relationship. Having those weak spots leaves one vulnerable to abuse on all levels. Working on your mental, internal, and external hurts; only makes you stronger in the long run and opens your eyes to potential red flags. Improving your health, physically and mentally, leads to you being able to do the things God needs you to do, and working on your finances, taking care of the blessings God has provided, helps you to be dependent on God alone!

The perfect example of a woman in preparation and focused on self, husband, children, and then the home is the Proverbs 31 woman. This woman was not only serving her purpose but also possessed some of the same qualities as Ruth. I have heard women say they want a financially stable man, and there is nothing wrong with that. They say they want a man who will care for them; again, nothing is wrong with that. I also hear women say a man must have "x, y, and z" before they even entertain him, but I ask what you are bringing in all your "glory" to the relationship.

Enters your example, the Proverbs 31 woman. You may disagree, which is okay, but if you are not on this level, sister, you have some work to do. This woman was on her hustle, not just for herself, but for the Lord, her husband, children, staff, and those she encountered. Proverbs 31:10-31, 10" A capable, intelligent, and virtuous woman- who is he who can find her?" Let's pause here. This first verse says a lot! Do you possess these qualities, or are you actively working on these qualities? You see, this is a woman who is developing in her faith, intelligent and able to do things for herself, and above all, virtuous! What is virtuous? According to Oxford languages, having or showing high moral standards, Merriam-Webster defines as "morally good." Again, is this you or the woman you are becoming and preparing to be?

Secondly, I think we all miss this; verse 10 says, who is he who can find her? Did you see it? We are sometimes so busy with the "looking for a man" mantra that we miss the man who has worked on himself and aligned with God, finding, or seeing us! Proverbs 31 verse 10 continues, "She is more precious than jewels and her value is far above rubies or pearls. The woman is compared to fine, precious jewels; however, she is above them all. Do you consider your worth above precious jewels?" Are you clearing out the clutter in your life to value yourself no matter what society says? Some of us need a life coach, a mentor, or therapy to help us address those areas that need pruning to push us to our greatness and purpose.

Proverbs verse 11, "The heart of her husband trusts in her confidently and relies on and believes in her securely so that he has no lack of [honest] gain or need of [dishonest] spoil." What will you bring to the relationship? What are you working on that will be an addition, a plus? What gain will your partner have when connected to you? If you cannot think of one or more, preparation mode and "Operation...fill in your name" is your main priority! Proverbs verse 12, "She comforts, encourages, and does him only good as long as there is life within her." In preparing yourself, you must be whole and able to motivate, comfort, and care for others. You must be able not to hold grudges and know how to communicate your feelings and needs in love.

Proverbs verses 13-16, 13" She seeks out wool and flax and works with willing hands [to develop it]. 14 She is like the merchant ships loaded with foodstuffs; she brings her household's food from a far [country]. 15 She rises while it is yet night and gets [spiritual] food for her household and assigns her maids their tasks. 16 She considers a [new] field before she buys *or* accepts it [expanding prudently and not courting neglect of her present duties by assuming other duties]; with her savings [of time and strength] she plants fruitful vines in her vineyard." Are you resourceful in preparation?

These verses speak to how you should prepare to care for your household and provide for the things you need, not want. It explains how you should manage your finances and be a good steward of what God has provided for you to care for and maintain. This preparation is not just for those wanting to be married but for every woman to live a fruitful and blessed life. Proverbs verses 17-20, 17 "She girds herself with strength [spiritual, mental, and physical fitness for her God-given task] and makes her arms strong and firm. 18 She tastes and sees that her gain from work [with and for God] is good; her lamp goes not out, but it burns on continually through the night [[of trouble, privation, or sorrow, warning away fear, doubt, and distrust]. 19 She lays her hands to the spindle, and her hands hold the distaff. 20 She opens her hand to the poor, yes, she reaches out her filled hands to the needy [whether in body, mind, or spirit]." As you prepare, you must serve your purpose for God and minister to others in need. A significant part of why we are here is to serve and live in, on, and with purpose!

The Proverbs 31 woman is a clear example of ensuring that you are whole, morally sound, faithful, and a servant. As you work to "gather" yourself or "put yourself together," stay focused on your WHY! You will need to be faithful, learn to serve others with God's blessing, and remain connected to God's word. In preparing and working on yourself, being used by God for his glory, you must stay focused on what you need to do to get to where you are healthy and thriving, setting yourself up for victory!

And finally, in Proverbs verses 21-31, 21, "She fears not the snow for her family, for all her household are doubly clothed in scarlet. 22 She makes for herself coverlets, cushions, and rugs of tapestry. Her clothing is linen, pure and fine, and of purple [such as that of which the clothing of the priests and the hallowed cloths of the temple were made]. 23 Her husband is known in the [city's] gates, when he sits among the elders of the land. 24 She makes fine linen garments and leads others to buy them; she delivers to the merchants girdles [or sashes that free one up for service]. 25 Strength and dignity are her clothing and her position is strong and secure; she rejoices over the future [the latter day or time to come, knowing that she and her family are in readiness for it]! 26 She opens her mouth in skillful and godly Wisdom, and on her tongue is the law of kindness [giving counsel and instruction]. 27 She looks well to how things go in her household, and the bread of idleness (gossip, discontent, and self-pity) she will not eat. 28 Her children rise up and call her blessed (happy, fortunate, and to be envied); and her husband boasts of and praises her, [saying] 29 Many daughters have done virtuously, nobly, and well [with the strength of character that is steadfast in goodness], but you excel them all. 30 Charm and grace are deceptive, and beauty is vain, [because it is not lasting], but a woman who reverently and worshipfully fears the Lord, she shall be praised! 31 Give her the fruit of her hands, and let her own works praise her in the gates [of the city]!"

Lastly, you must not succumb to fear as you prepare and build up yourself but remain faithful that God will help provide for your well-being. You must clothe yourself in modesty, respect, and excellence, and work diligently, not just on our purpose, but with what God has placed in your hands to succeed. You must work on your self-esteem and confidence, a running theme here, and walk in the assurance that you are more than enough and can achieve anything you envision. You must watch what you say and speak life to yourself and others. If marriage is your goal, your preparation should include how you will raise and care for your children, the relationship you will cultivate with them, and how you will support your husband and represent your household.

My attendance in a pre-marital class as a single woman with no prospect in sight was not by mistake! It was God's way of showing me what I needed to grow, work on, develop, and practice. He revealed that my priorities did not align with my purpose. It was God's way of saying, "Girl, get yourself together so I can bless you with what I have in store for you." Had I not been open to the Holy Spirit, I would have missed this opportunity when I needed it most! I would have kept focusing on my wants and desires that did not align with God's, which always equals disaster! Ruth and the Proverbs 31 woman have so much to teach us! They teach us how to be in a relationship with others and build a strong relationship with God!

Are you ready to go into your cocoon? Are you prepared to let go of what hurts you to develop your mental, emotional, and physical muscles to succeed? Are you willing to turn the inspection lens on to address your mess? Are you ready to prepare yourself to truly receive the goodness that God has in store for you?

Girl, Get Yourself Together!
Reflections

What makes you, you?

What are your strengths?

What are your weaknesses/insecurities?

Do you love yourself, in all your essence? Why or why not?
How will you need to improve your mental, emotional, physical, and financial wellness?

What does preparation mean and look like to you?

Read Proverbs 31: 10-31. What does the word reveal to you?

If marriage is your desire, what will a man gain in you as a wife right now? Think about your financial, mental, spiritual, emotional, and physical state and apply it to the question.

What is the kingdom gaining from you if marriage is not your desire? Think about your financial, mental, spiritual, emotional, and physical state and apply it to the question.

Chapter 6

Eyes on the Prize!

"Set your minds on things that are above, not on things that are on earth."
-Colossians 3:2

Keeping my mind stayed on Jesus!

Yes, Lord, yes! However, staying focused and obedient can be hard when you are single. I will not pretend that hormones do not get bothered and temptations arise because they do in REAL life but staying focused and obedient in our single season is vital because we must protect our spirit and body at all costs. The last chapter touched on working on and preparing yourself for your next during your single season, and doing so requires that you are focused, not just on your goals, but on the word of God and being obedient to what God is directing you to do. The business of staying focused and obedient does not mean you have to live a boring, dull life. No, it means setting, re-evaluating, and meeting your personal goals. It means understanding your purpose, working to fulfill it, and not becoming distracted by outside forces that steer you away from the care and protection of God.

Psalm 37:4-6, 4 "Delight yourself also in the Lord, and He will give you the desires and petitions of your heart. 5 Commit your way to the Lord [roll and repose each care of your load on Him]; trust (lean on, rely on, and be confident) also in Him and he will bring it to pass. 6, And He will make your uprightness and right standing with God go forth as the light, and your justice and right as [the shining sun of] the noonday." Our Father simply wants us to focus on Him and find joy in committing to His word and trusting that He will guide and lead us down the right path.

One of the ways I delighted and committed myself to the Lord was by joining the singles' ministry at my church. The singles' ministry was a huge step for me, but it grew me in ways I would have never grown had I not joined. I was able to develop relationships with other single women who understood where I was and was able to pray for and hold me accountable. I became very active in the ministry and served others, which took the focus from being "alone" and not dating to developing skills that I still use to minister to others today. I joined and eventually became the leader of a singles' small group, and although I argued with God about it, it helped me stay focused on God's word and promises. I even went so far as to create a small notebook of scriptures to reflect and meditate on when I felt my flesh trying to take over and lead me to disaster. I remained faithful to the small group and was obedient in taking charge of the lessons and studying to prepare each week. And in this time of focus and obedience, I could see how God was molding and preparing me for what was to come.

Keeping your eyes on the prize is important because when you do not keep your mind and heart connected to God, your flesh will take control, which will not make your way prosperous. Amid being prayerful, studying my word, faithful to my small group and ministry, and serving others, I fell hard. I experienced heartache and the loss of a potential new life. I allowed my flesh to have its way, which was not worth it. It led to feelings of regret, conviction, and depression. I felt ashamed and unworthy of being a leader. How could I be a leader when I let myself become unfocused? I distanced myself from my group, friends, and family. I allowed negative thoughts about myself to run wild and felt like

Hester Prynne in the Scarlet Letter. It was not until I allowed myself to hear from God again that I understood all that had happened and why.

God honestly does not want to harm us, but He will use disobedience as a lesson to turn us back to Him. In the deep, God allowed me to see that my flesh did what it would always do when I took my focus off Him. I allowed myself to engage with someone I knew did not want to be in a relationship with me. I felt shame for being this "Christian" single woman pregnant by someone I knew did not want more. I prayed for God to remove my hurt and guilt because I did not want to face the truth of living outside the will of God. Still, God answered me by saying all life was precious, no matter how it came about, and with repentance and asking God to forgive me, I felt peace with being a single mother, and then, just like that, after accepting what would have been my future, I miscarried.

I was never angry with God, but it took me months to crawl out of the hole of depression, not be mad and forgive myself. At 13, my doctor told me that creating life would be hard for me because of my "wonderful" reproductive system. Here I was, pregnant and not happy about it. How ungrateful? By December of 2009, I had had long talks with God and my journal, and on New Year's Eve, the Holy Spirit told me enough was enough! That was the last night I wallowed in my misery. I forgave myself and recommitted my focus and obedience back to God.

When I allowed God to use me, my focus became less about what I wanted, although the desire was there, to what God needed from me to do His will. In this time of preparation, focus, and obedience, there were challenges, temptations, victories, and losses. I learned and gained but never lost focus. I tried and failed but picked myself back up again to start over. Being focused and obedient will be met with failure because we are not perfect, but our heart, willingness, repentance, and recommitment are all God needs to place us back on our path. Again, God is not out to get us. He wants what is best for us to succeed here on earth. But to do so means giving up those worldly desires and doing as Psalm 119:15-16 says 15, "I will meditate on Your precepts and respect Your ways [the paths of life marked out by Your law]. 16 I will delight in Your statues; I will not forget Your word."

Keeping your eyes on the prize is focusing on the word, meditating on it, and praying daily for God to direct you in all you do. Our single season is one of devotion and obedience. It is allowing God to use you, as you are "free" from other "duties" as that of a wife. 1 Corinthians 7:34, "And the unmarried woman or girl is concerned *and* anxious about the matters of the Lord, how to be wholly separated *and* set apart in body and in spirit." It is understanding your calling and developing the skills you need to serve others. It is learning to *hear* from and listen to the Holy Spirit. It is intentionally focusing on personal and spiritual growth and healing. And if becoming a wife and mother is your desire, you must understand what submissive means. It is placing your focus on how to care for your home and finances. It is unlearning what was toxic in your upbringing so that you may raise your children in the ways of the Lord.

Keeping your eyes on the prize and being obedient is finding accountability partners who are non-judgmental and grounded in the word. We need accountability partners who will correct and pray for us, tell us the truth, no matter how horrible it feels, and stand in the gap for us when they see trouble on the way. Deuteronomy 5:33 demonstrates keeping your eyes on the prize and its rewards, verse 33, "You shall walk in all the ways which the Lord your God has commanded you, that you may live and that it may be well with you and that you may live long in the land which you will possess" and James 1:22, states, 22 "But the doers of the Word [obey the message], and not merely listeners to it, betraying yourselves [into deception by reasoning contrary to the Truth]."

As I stated before, being single is not for the faint of heart, and keeping our focus and obedience to God's word is a daily commitment. I believe that when you focus on God and surround yourself with accountability partners, keeping your eyes on the prize will not be difficult. How can you get started? You can join a ministry working aligned with your spiritual gifts, commit to prayer and a bible study schedule, and set immediate goals. Yes, there will be days, maybe weeks or months, where you may not be on your "A game," but when you have all your ducks in a row to help you along the way, you can bounce back to get back on track!

Eyes on the Prize
Reflections

Do you know what your purpose is? If so, how are you working on it? If not, what gift (spiritual) are you using to serve the kingdom?

What does obedience to God's word look like in your life?

What does "keeping your eyes on the prize" mean to you?

Think of a time when you were unfocused or disobedient. What was the outcome, and how did you recover?

Find three verses to meditate on when you feel challenged by your flesh.

Bible Verse 1:

Bible Verse 2:

Bible Verse 3:

List 3-4 ways to be focused and obedient to God's word.

Chapter 7

Patience is a Virtue

"Patience is not the ability to wait but how you act while you're waiting."
-Joyce Meyer

All good things take time to prepare

Patience, what does it mean? According to Oxford Languages, patience is the capacity to accept or tolerate delay, trouble, or suffering without getting angry or upset. Synonyms include resignation, composure, calmness, restraint, tolerance, forbearance, and tranquility, just to name a few. But what does the bible say about patience as one of the fruits of the Spirit? Galatians 5:22-23, 22 "But the fruit of the [Holy] Spirit [the work which His presence within accomplishes] is love, joy (gladness), peace, patience (an even temper, forbearance), kindness, goodness (benevolence), faithfulness, 23 Gentleness (meekness, humility), self-control (self-restraint, continence). Against such things, there is no law [that can bring a charge]." According to the world, having patience is the ability to accept, be okay with, and tolerate delay or something that causes trouble without getting upset, meaning having the ability to compose yourself, to keep yourself grounded and settled during whatever is going on.

Let's look at this example of patience. You go to the store to purchase some items, and now it is time to pay; however, there are only three registers open, the lines are super long, and you must be somewhere in 30 minutes on the other side of town. Now due to your time crunch, you must exercise patience. You must accept this delay without becoming upset. You must compose yourself and remain calm. I know many of us would probably lose it or become frustrated, but in this scenario, how you choose to *wait* will dictate the next few minutes of your life and reveal the areas that need to improve.

What if you are sick and show up to your appointment on time; however, you wait an hour before someone acknowledges you? How would you "act" or show patience in this situation?

Let's look again at patience in the bible. The KJV uses the word longsuffering. The Amplified Bible, as quoted above, elaborates to say an even temper and forbearance. Finally, the Amplified version on my bible app elaborates by stating, "not the ability to wait, but how we act while waiting." Oxford Languages define *longsuffering* as having or showing patience in spite of troubles, especially those caused by other people. These three definitions explain one word differently, but all say the same thing. Patience is not in the "waiting," the act of it, meaning it is not the capacity or ability to wait something out, but it is all about what we do in the "wait" and how we respond.

Patience is all about composure or how you react while waiting, which directly correlates to our preparation time. During our season of singleness, many women tend to be impatient regarding relationships. We rush into them because we do not want to be alone and make rash decisions about allowing a man to engage us sexually, yes, when we should take our time. We make many hasty decisions because we are tired of waiting, the actual verb. We become fed up with going out with our girls and make these poor decisions because we want romance, date night, surprise gifts, and to post our perfect pictures with the hashtag #relationshipgoals.

However, James 1: 3-4, 3 "Be assured *and* understand that the trial *and* proving of your faith bring out endurance *and* steadfastness *and* patience. 4 But let endurance *and* steadfastness *and* patience have full play *and* do a thorough work, so that you may be [people] perfectly and fully developed [with no defects], lacking nothing." There it is! Right there in the word! Patience during our single season is the time to work on ourselves. In preparation, we are doing what the definition of patience says. We are maturing and actively repairing areas of our lives that need healing. If marriage is your goal or even a healthy relationship, determine who you are, what you need, and what you will not entertain. It is developing a prayer life and learning to allow God to lead. It is serving our purpose and learning to use our gifts to glorify God and the kingdom. It is becoming healthy physically, emotionally, spiritually, and mentally.

While we wait, we must use this time to visualize and be clear about our future. After attending that premarital class, my wait began to look different. I used the time to focus on what I needed to correct and re-establish in my life. I implemented boundaries that allowed me to stay out of toxic relationships. I became more aware of people's intentions and nurtured my gift of discernment. I focused on hearing God more, allowing Him to lead me, and began writing notes for my first book. I joined my father in establishing our church and then creating our radio and online ministry.

I became debt-free, built my first home, and was the SUPER aunt! I started working on my purpose, which led to a girls' mentoring group, and I became a speaker that uplifts women and those in the school counseling field. I began to travel and published my first book. I stayed the course, connected to God, and decided to enjoy life! I dated here and there and was quick to dismiss them too. Why? Because I allowed God to lead and direct me. God nurtured my discernment and guided me. Was I bamboozled a few times? Of course, I was because the enemy always knows how to disguise itself, but once found out, to the curb, that person went! I also began working on myself physically, eating differently, and becoming content!

Woah! That's a big word! CONTENT! How many of you are CONTENT? How many of you are ready to rest in contentment? Content, as defined by Oxford Languages:

adj-
1. in a state of peaceful happiness.
2. Willing to accept a particular thing; satisfied.

verb-
1. satisfy (someone).
2. accept as adequate despite wanting more or better.

noun-
1. a state of satisfaction.

I became content with the wait! I became satisfied with where I was in life. I accepted where I was and stopped comparing my life to others and what I saw because, to be truthful, being single is not a terrible lot in life as people try to make it out to be. I became more than okay with where I was and what God was doing for me and through me. I had finally realized that whether I stayed single or got into a relationship, either way, I was more than good! I was living out Philippians 4:11-12!

Philippians verse 11-12 reads, "Not that I am implying that I was in any personal want, for I have learned how to be content (satisfied or disquieted) in whatever state I am. 12 I know how to be abased *and* live humbly in straitened circumstances difficult times], and I know also how to enjoy plenty *and* live in abundance. I have learned in all circumstances the secret of facing every situation, whether well-fed or going hungry, whether sufficiency *and* enough to spare or going without *and* being in want."

I had actualized what James 1:3-4 said. I endured the moments of want and turned that into focusing on God! I allowed my endurance and steadfastness to perfect me into a better me. I was so content that I told my mother that if I never got married, I was okay with it and asked her and my father to help me become a foster parent. Y'all, I was full and satisfied! Why? Because I was working on my purpose and pursuing the things God wanted me to bring into focus. I stopped caring about what the world had to say and became content and filled with peace with where God was taking me on my journey.

To become content, you must shut out the noise from relatives, friends, and societal expectations. You must arrive at a place of knowing who you are and what gives you joy, not happiness. You must align your thoughts, ways, and purpose with God. You must develop a healthy devotional and study time to meditate and hear from God. You must decide to live life unapologetically without regrets! You must develop this fruit of the Spirit because it applies to more than just your single status but also your work, career aspirations, family, health victories, finances, and emotional and mental healing. Patience is the building up of your character when faced with many obstacles because, to be honest, life is full of drama and obstacles, and knowing when to move forward. Patience is what you do in the waiting and not the act of waiting! And finally, patience is the muscle that will help to build your faith!

Patience is a Virtue
Reflections

What does “have patience” mean to you outside the formal definitions of patience?

In what areas of your life do you need patience?

What are some things you need to work on while you “wait”?

What does “being in a place of contentment” mean to you?

Are you content with your life? If yes, why? If not, why not?

As a single woman, how will you choose to live your life from this day forward?

Chapter 8

Building my Faith Muscle

"Faith is made up of three things: knowledge, belief, and trust."
-Spurgeon, C. H.

I am standing on the word of God; my faith will carry me through.

Saying this is sometimes easier said than done. Oxford Languages defines faith as:

Noun-
1. complete trust or confidence in someone or something.
2. strong belief in God or in the doctrines of a religion, based on spiritual apprehension rather than proof.
·a system of religious beliefs
·a strongly held belief or theory.

Faith, in terms of religion, is knowing what God is capable and able to do in our life. It is standing on the knowledge from examples in the bible that gives us the strength to keep going. The illustrations show us people with unwavering faith that God would provide, heal, remove, raise from the dead, protect, and bless them. Faith is an absolute knowing that God will get us through our ups and downs. We believe or have confidence in what we know of God, and we trust that knowledge to know and believe things will come to pass.

As a single woman, I always have faith that God will one day bless me with what I have prayed for and that my tears, anger, hurt, and pain of failed relationships, friendships, dating experiences, and career woes will be all worth it. But, due to some of my experiences, I became doubtful because of the hassle and drama, which often led to being exhausted, hurt, disappointed, and I felt like giving up. Therefore, I knew I had to change my mindset and focus on the word of God by incorporating affirmations. An affirmation is the action or process of affirming something or being affirmed (Oxford Languages). I write affirmations affirming who I am in Christ, whom I want to be, what I will and will not do, and what God has done for me. Affirmations allow you to speak with faith, declaring what you are standing in, believing for, and speaking into life. It is growing and exercising your faith muscle and is working your faith as James 2: 20 says, "Are you willing to be shown [proof], you foolish (unproductive, spiritually deficient) fellow, that faith apart from [good] works is inactive *and* ineffective *and worthless*?"

Speaking your affirmation is your good work. It is you bringing your faith alive. It is you seeing it before it happens. It is you standing on the word of God. It shows God that you trust him to work it out in your favor. As a single woman focused on purpose, ministry, and growth, your everyday affirmation is faith in God blessing you with what you have prayed for that aligns with what He desires for you.

Maturing in your faith walk during your single season is developing a solid study and prayer life and entrusting God to lead you when you do not know which way to go. What would you say if I were to ask you how your study and prayer life looked? Do you actively dedicate time to praying each day? How often do you study? I know I had to commit and dedicate time to studying intentionally. I had to lose the excuse of being too tired or not having time. I had to create a calendar event for a specific day and time and let others know about my committed day so they would not interrupt me. I prayed and asked God to lead me in what to study and to illuminate the word as I read so that I would know how to use it in my daily walk. I meditated on scriptures and used them throughout the week, which helped my faith walk. Studying is crucial because it provides evidence of God's divine power, love, and grace. It shows you what God can and is ready to do in your life. It offers faith and hope! Studying the word of God is part one of your secret sauce to success and maturing in your faith walk.

Now when we combine the second part, praying, we are setting the scene for victory in our single season. Praying is one way of speaking in faith! When we pray, we are not just praying for what we desire, need, or want from God. We are conversing with God and giving His word back to Him in faith and assurance for what we believe God will do for us. It recounts what God is doing, has done, and is praising and giving thanks to Him in advance. It is praying to be used for His glory and purpose and is our way to worship Him. Praying is how we show our faith in God's word. Every day I pray and thank God for a new day. I pray, asking for forgiveness and redirection, and give praise for His grace, mercy, and lovingkindness. I pray and thank Him for what has already been given to me in heavenly place according to Ephesians 1:3, "May blessing (praise, laudation, and eulogy) be to the God and father of our Lord Jesus Christ (the Messiah) Who has blessed us *in Christ* with every spiritual (given by the Holy Spirit) blessing in the heavenly realm!" I pray and thank God for my heart's desire and for those desires to be in His will. I pray and thank God for my blessing and glorify who He is.

Our prayers and study time are simply our faith in constant action. It is us gaining knowledge of God's word, believing in it, and trusting God to do what He says He will do. One book I want to highlight to help build your faith is 1 Samuel 1:5-18 and 1Samuel 2: 19-20. The story of Hannah and her prayer. Hannah's story applies to any area of life you are praying for in faith. Hannah wanted to conceive a child but was barren, but she did not allow that to deter her belief that God would provide for her. Hannah prayed specifically and with intent, and she prayed to return her blessing to God, and Hannah conceived! Praying in faith is not just believing, trusting, and receiving from God. It shows God, through faith, that what He blesses us with will be used to uplift and grow His kingdom. Faith without works is dead! Our action of praying, believing, and trusting is our faith in action! Our daily, weekly, or monthly affirmations speak faith and what we declare and believe in the atmosphere.

Learning to be faithful and exercising faith during our time of preparation, focus, being obedient, and how we wait prepares us for what is next. Being single is not a curse; it is your time to shine. It is your time to learn what is and is not good for you, grow mentally and spiritually, create, set, and implement boundaries, heal through therapy, know who you are, and be comfortable in your skin. It is your time to pursue the things of God and serve in ministry. It is time to be content and exercise faith because you are showing God you trust where He has you at a particular time in your life and with what you have.

Winning in your singleness is being victorious in the stages God and life will take you through. Winning in your singleness builds your spiritual gifts to use in all your relationships. Winning in your singleness creates space and time for God to have His way in your life.

Winning in your singleness in simply relying on FAITH to get you through! Winning in your singleness is being knowledgeable of God's word, believing in the word, and trusting God to do what He does best, BLESS! Some of you may desire relationships that will lead to marriage. Some of you are divorced and are reacclimating yourself to single life. Some of you are widowed, pressing through grief and being "alone" again, and some of you are at peace with being single. No matter your stage or season during your singleness, know that building a relationship with the Father is vital, NOT waiting on your Boaz!

Building my Faith Muscle
Reflections

What does faith look like to you?

What areas do you need to mature in faith?

Give two examples of how God has been faithful in your life.

How does your study and prayer time look?

If you do not have time dedicated to studying and prayer, what can you do to implement a consistent time in your schedule?
Find three faith scriptures you can meditate on to help build your faith in God's word.

Scripture 1:

Scripture 2:

Scripture 3:

AFFIRMATIONS

I believe affirmations are vital in developing our faith. Below are sentence starters for you to write an affirmation. Write an affirmation for your season of singleness and attach scripture to the declaration. Always give God back His word!

Sentence starters:

I will be free from…

I am bold in the Lord...

I declare that…

I will not…

I will…

I have…

God is…

God will…

I am…

My Affirmation:

Scripture:

My Affirmation:

Scripture:

Overcomer Affirmation

I am an overcomer! I have the victory! What God has for me is for me, and no one can take it from me! I will not feel defeated and will not persecute myself for my mistakes. I will speak the word of God over my circumstances. I will declare the word of God in my life. I will be more than a conqueror! God will be my refuge, and in Him will I trust. I will not lean on my understanding but entrust God to reveal what paths and directions to take. I will not allow the devil to overtake my mind but meditate on the word to breathe life into my spirit. I will not fall into despair. I will walk in FAITH, trusting with no doubt. I will rejoice in trials, for my praise will help me to press my way through. I will give thanks to Jehovah Shalom, who is my peace! I am an overcomer! I have the victory! I am more than a conqueror!

Isaiah 54:17

"But no weapon that is formed against me shall prosper, and every tongue that shall rise against you in judgment you shall show to be in the wrong. This [peace, righteousness, security, triumph over opposition] is the heritage of the servants of the Lord [those in whom the ideal Servant of the Lord is reproduced]; this is the righteousness *or* the vindication which they obtain from Me [this is that which I impart to them as their justification], says the Lord."

Father God, I thank you for the daughters who will receive this book. Thank you for this seed, and pray the word falls on fertile ground.

~Your Prayer~

Lord, thank you for being you! Thank you for your incredible power and glorious works! Lord, forgive my sins and continue showing me where I fall short. Lord, I pray to hear your voice. I pray that your word will illuminate and sown into my heart. Lord, I pray for your blessing during this season. Lord, heal my heart, cover my mind, protect me, and give me strength when I feel I cannot move forward. Father, your word renews and restores, and I pray you are renewing my heart and mind and restoring hope and purpose! Father, thank you for being the Lord of Peace. I need your peace to surround and live in me. Lord, I pray for a release from bondage when I feel trapped by circumstances. Holy Spirit, comfort me!

I pray that your message will help me heal! Lord, help me to understand your word and allow the reflection questions to show me where I need growth! Lord, I pray that you will restore my confidence and that I will learn to love myself as you love me! I pray, Lord, that you will hone my focus and help me to be obedient to your word. Lord, I pray that you will build my character, hope, and trust in you during the wait. Lord, help me to pursue purpose and serve in ministry. Father, I thank you for your son, Jesus! I thank you for the blood that was shed and plead the blood of Jesus over my mind and heart. In

Jesus's name, I pray. AMEN!

ABOUT THE AUTHOR

Dedra D. Colston is a native of Dallas, TX, and the voice and founder of Infiniteeworks. She is an Author, Professional Development Speaker, Professional School Counselor, and Consultant with 22 years of experience in public education. Dedra was the Co-host of Kingdom Talk, an online Christian radio station, and spent several years leading a singles' small group for her church. She published her first devotional, "Live. Learn. Grow. A Spiritual and Personal Growth Journey," in 2018 and is the co-founder of the Diamond Girls Mentoring Program. Dedra believes in EMPOWERING women and girls to walk in PURPOSE and LOVE, which led to the development of "Not Waiting on my Boaz." She is dedicated to pouring into women and girls and looks for opportunities to do so! Dedra is a daughter, sister, aunt, line sister, and soror. In June of 2022, Dedra married her childhood friend, now her best friend and husband! The two are enjoying their new status and look forward to God's blessings!

~NOTES~

www.ingramcontent.com/pod-product-compliance
Lightning Source LLC
LaVergne TN
LVHW040951150826
845672LV00002B/634

* 9 7 9 8 8 4 6 5 5 9 7 1 4 *